Contents

Some words appear in bold, **like this**. You can find out what they mean in "Words to know" on page 23.

A balanced diet

A **balanced diet** includes fruit, vegetables, **starchy foods**, milk and **dairy foods**, meat, fish, eggs, and beans.

fruit and vegetables

starchy foods

meat, fish, eggs, and beans

sugar and fat

milk and dairy foods

The **eatwell plate** shows us the main food groups. You need to eat food from these food groups and get plenty of exercise to keep your body healthy.

Fruit

vine

Fruit grows on plants. Apples, tomatoes, and raspberries are fruits. Apples grow on trees. Some tomatoes grow on vines. Raspberries grow on bushes. Eating fruit helps your body fight illness and keeps you healthy.

Always wash fruit before you eat it.

Most fruits can be picked and eaten as they are. Sometimes fruits are squeezed and made into juice. Most children need to eat 5 servings of fruit and vegetables each day.

Vegetables

peas

A vegetable is a type of plant. Carrots and peas are vegetables. Carrots grow under the ground. Peas grow above the ground. Eating vegetables helps keep your body healthy.

broccoli

Always wash vegetables before you eat them.

Some vegetables can be picked and eaten as they are. Some vegetables are cooked. Most children need to eat 5 servings of vegetables and fruit each day.

Starchy foods

oat

oats

Starchy foods include pasta, bread, potatoes, and food made from **grains**. Grains are the seeds from some plants. Oats, wheat, and rice are grains. Eating starchy foods gives you **energy** and keeps you healthy.

pasta

bread

We make some grains into flour. Bread, pasta, and buns are made from flour. Other grains, such as rice, are cooked in water. Make sure that at least half of the grains you eat are made from whole grains.

Milk and dairy foods

milk

Cows make milk. Many farmers use machines to take milk from the cows. They take the milk to a **dairy**. Machines at the dairy prepare the milk. Then the milk is put into bottles or cartons.

cheese

yoghurt

Milk can be made into **dairy foods**. Cheese and yoghurt are dairy foods. Eating dairy foods helps build strong bones and teeth.

Meat, fish, eggs, and beans

Meat is a food that comes from animals such as cows, pigs, and chickens. Meat, fish, and eggs give you **protein**. Other foods that give you protein are beans and nuts.

Most meat is cooked before it can be eaten. It is important to cook meat well. Eating protein helps you to grow.

Healthy fats

Some fats in our food are good for us. Some fats are bad for us if we eat too much of them. Healthy fats are found in fish, seeds, nuts, and plants. Unhealthy fats are found in cakes, biscuits, and fried food.

16

oil

Oils are fats. Some oils come from vegetables or seeds. Some people use oil when they cook food. Oils can also be used on salads. Eating some of these oils helps you fight illness and stay healthy.

Sugar

There is a lot of sugar in biscuits, sweets, fizzy drinks, and cakes. Too much sugar is bad for your body. To keep your body healthy, you should try to eat only small amounts of sugar.

Too much sugar is bad for your teeth. It is important to brush your teeth after eating sugary foods. You need to clean the sugar from your teeth.

Exercise and sleep

As well as eating a **balanced diet**, your body needs regular **exercise**. Regular exercise helps build strong bones and muscles, and a healthy heart.

Your body also needs to rest. Sleep helps you stay strong and healthy. Most children need between 10 and 12 hours of sleep each night.

Can you remember?

Can you guess which food groups these foods belong to? Look back through the book if you need help.

Answers on page 24

Words to know

balanced diet diet that includes food from all the food groups. A balanced diet helps keep a body healthy and fit.

dairy place where butter and cheese are made from milk

dairy food food made from milk. Cheese, yoghurt, butter, and cream are dairy foods.

eatwell plate the eatwell plate shows us what foods to eat to stay healthy

energy power to do something. We need energy when we work or play.

exercise physical activity that helps keep a body healthy and fit

grains seeds of some plants. Wheat and rice are grains.

oil fat in food

protein substance in food that gives the body energy and helps it grow. Eggs, meat, nuts, and beans have protein in them.

starchy food food that gives the body energy. Pasta, cereals, and bread are starchy foods.

Index

Answers to quiz on page 22:
a) fruit b) vegetables c) starchy foods d) milk e) meat f) fat

Notes for parents and teachers

Before reading

Show the children the photo of the eatwell plate on p. 4. Guide children in a discussion about what "balanced" means. Then explain that a balanced diet includes food from all the food groups. Tell children they will learn about the main food groups.

After reading

- As a shared task with the class, write down as many foods as the children can think of in each food group. Ask children if they can think of any foods that are not so healthy.
- Bring in a selection of food magazines (such as free supermarket magazines). Ask children to find and cut out pictures of foods from different food groups and put them in separate piles. Give each child a paper plate and ask them to select a picture from each pile to put on their plates to make a healthy meal. Make a wall display of the children's healthy meals.